Brief Notes

THE LEASE AND ITS LANGUAGE

The publications in *Brief Notes* are outlines of core topics of interest to professionals involved in shopping center management. The outlines are capsule overviews of each topic. Many key points are covered, and shopping center examples are provided for further illustration. Core concepts in each area guide you on topics you may want to explore further. Each outline also contains a helpful glossary.

Brief Notes is designed to provide a helpful and informative overview of the topics covered. It is not intended to be a substitute for more extensive learning that can be achieved through attending ICSC educational programs and reading additional ICSC professional publications.

The outlines contained in *Brief Notes: Shopping Center Management:*

- Management Overview
- Finance
- Insurance and Risk Management
- The Lease and Its Language
- Leasing Strategies
- Maintenance
- Marketing
- Retailing
- Security

Brief Notes

THE LEASE AND ITS LANGUAGE

 International Council of Shopping Centers
New York

ABOUT THE INTERNATIONAL COUNCIL OF SHOPPING CENTERS

The International Council of Shopping Centers (ICSC) is the trade association of the shopping center industry. Serving the shopping center industry since 1957, ICSC is a not-for-profit organization with over 44,000 members in 77 countries worldwide.

ICSC members include shopping center

- owners
- developers
- managers
- marketing specialists
- leasing agents
- retailers
- researchers
- attorneys

- architects
- contractors
- consultants
- investors
- lenders and brokers
- academics
- public officials

ICSC sponsors more than 200 meetings a year and provides a wide array of services and products for shopping center professionals, including deal making events, conferences, educational programs, accreditation, awards, publications and research data.

For more information about ICSC, write or call the
International Council of Shopping Centers
1221 Avenue of the Americas
New York, NY 10020-1099
Telephone: 646-728-3800
Fax: 212-589-5555
info@icsc.org
http://www.icsc.org

This publication is designed to provide accurate and authoritative information in regard to the subject matter covered. It is sold with the understanding that the publisher is not engaged in rendering legal, accounting, or other professional services. If legal advice or other expert assistance is required, the services of a competent professional person should be sought.

—From a Declaration of Principles jointly adopted by
a Committee of the American Bar Association and a
Committee of Publishers.

Companies, professional groups, clubs and other organizations may qualify for special terms when ordering quantities of more than 20 of this title.

Published by
International Council of Shopping Centers
Publications Department
1221 Avenue of the Americas
New York, NY 10020-1099

ICSC Catalog No.: 242

ISBN: 1-58268-028-0

Contents

Preface

A shopping center has a complex set of relationships among tenants, landlords and lenders. These relationships are governed by the shopping center lease.

A shopping center manager who is knowledgeable about the lease and understands its importance can successfully resolve or prevent the conflicts that may arise from the different interests represented at the shopping center.

In addition to the lease, management of the shopping center frequently requires familiarity with other legal documents, including estoppel letters, nondisturbance agreements, construction documents and lease exhibits—all of which are explained in the following text.

Leases and legal language can be intimidating to persons unfamiliar with the meaning of the lease terms. However, the following pages simplify the language and explain the key points that will help you—the shopping center professional—understand the most important lease provisions and how they work in practice. Key words and terms are clearly defined, and listed in the glossary.

Acknowledgments

The material in this outline is based in part on a course presented at the International Council of Shopping Centers (ICSC) John T. Riordan School for Professional Development Management and Leasing Institutes.

The International Council of Shopping Centers gratefully acknowledges the individuals and companies mentioned below, who have contributed their expertise to this publication.

Andrew D. Small, Partner, Katten, Muchin, Zavis, Rosenman
Barnett P. Ruttenberg

Core Concepts

✓ Lessor
✓ Lessee
✓ Lender's role in the lease

THE PARTIES INVOLVED

From a legal perspective, a lease has the following main components:

- It serves as a conveyance of real property. Accordingly, like a deed, it is governed by general property law.
- It also serves as a contract, with provisions governed by general contract law.

The major purpose of a lease is to allocate risk, in advance, among all the parties involved in the lease. It should:

- Outline the responsibilities and obligations of the parties and provide solutions to typical issues.

- Specify, from a drafting and resolutions perspective, that the party (or entity) that controls the situation or outcome is responsible for remedying the situation.

The interests of many parties are represented in a lease. Generally, these include:

- The owner: The owner may be any form of legal entity—a corporation, a partnership (either general or limited) or a sole proprietorship. The owner or landlord is typically referred to in a lease as the lessor.
- The manager: The manager acts on the behalf of the owner or landlord to operate the shopping center and to enforce the terms of the lease.
- The leasing representative: The leasing representative can be an agent, broker or work directly for the management company of the shopping center or the retailer. The role of the leasing representative is to negotiate the terms of the lease among other tasks, which involves site selection in the case of the retailer or prospecting in the case of the landlord.
- The lenders: The types of lenders who may have an interest in the terms of the lease are:

  —With respect to the landlords, construction lenders, who finance the building of the project and have an interest in making certain that landlords meet their cash flow obligations and so qualify for a permanent loan
  —The "take out" lender or permanent lender, who typically finances the project once it is built, and also has an interest in making certain that landlords can meet their cash flow obligations.
  —With respect to the tenant, lenders who finance inventory or the cost of the tenant's operation or the cost of

the tenant's initial construction may have an interest in the lease.

■ The tenant: Different tenants may have different interests in the lease, depending upon their size or the role they play within the center. For example, anchor tenants may expect to alter their store hours for special midnight sales. A small tenant may want assurance that an anchor store will operate in a manner that will draw customer traffic to the shopping center. The tenant is typically referred to in a lease as the lessee.

Role of Center Manager

Typically, the shopping center manager will be the first person involved in resolving any ambiguities in a lease. Therefore, the manager's familiarity with the center's leases can be critical to the avoidance or resolution of potential conflict at the shopping center.

Role of the Courts

Because it is difficult to accurately predict the outcome of a judicial ruling or the enforcement of a violation, it is important to carefully outline and review all the details of the shopping center lease for uniformity in each clause. It is very important to make certain that one clause in the lease does not contradict another.

Core Concepts

✓ LOI
✓ Binding or not binding
✓ Detailed or broad language

LETTERS OF INTENT

Letters of intent (LOI) are generally nonbinding documents submitted prior to a formal lease. Although not usually legally enforceable in most jurisdictions in the U.S., they tend to be moral obligations that lay out in advance the terms on which the parties agree. Some documents are very specific. For example, in a letter of intent the terms of the construction allowance usually would only state the amount the landlord would contribute but not when that sum would be paid. The letter of intent might also specify that the construction allowance could be used only to construct 30 feet of linear wall, a counter and air conditioning.

Although not binding, the letter of intent can be used as a basis for damages in a court of law. For example, a tenant can go to a judge and say, "Your Honor, I spent $100,000 on preconstruction fees. I had a letter of intent and the landlord led me on to prepare for use of the space. We had every intention to go through with the deal. The landlord chose to make the deal with one of my competitors for $10 per square foot more than we agreed to pay. Therefore, because of this signed letter of intent from the landlord, I expect the landlord to at least reimburse my costs for all of my efforts and good faith."

Letters of intent are not options on property because no consideration is exchanged between the parties and they are typically lacking in sufficient detail. Consideration usually is expressed in terms of exchange of money between the parties of a transaction. Without consideration there is generally no legally binding contract.

Letters of intent are usually used at the completion of the negotiation process between the landlord's leasing agent and the retailer's leasing representative as a confirmation of business terms. If these terms—now in writing—are agreed to by both parties, the lease document is prepared, usually by an attorney working for the shopping center owner. The representative of the tenant may then negotiate again, this time using the lease language.

Letters of intent are instruments sometimes used in the negotiation process. They may be presented in the following ways:

- Detailed language: There may be advantages to letters of intent with detailed language. For example, sometimes major issues are not carefully addressed, and this imprecise language results in a more lengthy negotiation process. Generally, when using a letter of intent as a tool in the negotiation process, it is best to use precise language.

■ Broad language: There may be advantages to letters of intent with broad language. For example, sometimes a lease can be negotiated with a handshake on the golf course. Sometimes you may be more comfortable letting each party's attorney negotiate the details. In this case, the role of an attorney as mediator, or the last word, can be an important tool of negotiation. It is possible to remain on friendly terms, for instance, and tell a party that you must keep a clause intact because your attorney has advised it.

Core Concepts

✓ Ambiguous lease clause

LEASE FORMS

The common ways to prepare shopping center lease forms are:

- Preprinted forms: Typesetting may have the advantage of appearing to be authoritative, which sometimes discourages changes by some tenants. Changes in this type of document are typically made in the margin of each paragraph. Sometimes an addendum of changes is attached to the document on a separate page.
- Computer-generated forms: Changes in the original document can be made easily from a computer disk.

Any lease document that invites several different interpretations may be dangerous to the interests of the landlord and the tenant. Generally, when a lease clause is ambiguous, rulings in court are made against a person who drafted the document. Therefore, it is very important to carefully review your lease form in order to eliminate any potential misinterpretations.

Core Concepts

✓ Lease clause
✓ Lease provision

PROVISIONS OF THE LEASE

The information that follows in this outline is intended to broaden the definitions in the lease as well as provide limited examples of the importance of a specific clause or illustrate its common usage.

Core Concepts

✓ Credit worthy tenant
✓ Lessee's entity: Is parent company or an affiliate without assets?

PARTIES TO THE LEASE

The parties to a shopping center lease are the landlord and the entity seeking space in the center. Each has specific requirements:

- Landlords want to be satisfied that the party with whom they are entering into a lease agreement is creditworthy and can comply with the lease. For example, a letter of intent may be negotiated with a parent corporation, but a lease may be submitted by an affiliate of the parent corporation. Carefully compare the name on the letter of intent and the name on the lease. If the lease is negotiated with the intent that the parent corporation will bear financial responsibility, you want to make certain that you are clearly dealing with the same party and can expect the financial resources that were originally represented.

■ Tenants want to be confident that the landlord from whom they are leasing is a responsible party. For example, some U.S. states have land trusts that may protect the landlord from liability. Therefore, if a tenant enters into a lease agreement with a land trust, the shopping center owner has no personal liability (with respect to the lease). Moreover, in most other cases, the landlord will attempt to contractually excuse itself from liability.

Core Concepts

✓ Name on storefront as opposed to corporation name

✓ Trade name sometimes implies upscale or popular price focus

TENANT'S TRADE NAME

The landlord must approve the trade name used by a tenant. The following considerations apply:

■ The name should convey the right image for the shopping center.

■ The tenant should not be allowed to change its trade name without the consent of the landlord. A landlord will often allow a trade name change if the tenant also changes the name of its other stores nationally or in a region. A tenant's name change may have a significant impact on the store's sales. If the landlord collects a percentage of the store's sales as a part of the rental (see Percentage

Rent under Rent), the landlord has a vested interest in the tenant's profitability and, hence, in the tenant's name.

- Some retail companies operate various concepts, each with its own focus and customer appeal. Some are upscale, some not. A company held responsible under the lease can significantly impact the store operation with a change in merchandise and store name. For example, Ann Taylor Inc. operates Ann Taylor and Ann Taylor Loft, two different stores. Abercrombie & Fitch operates Abercrombie & Fitch and Abercrombie, also two different stores. Gap, Inc. operates Gap, Banana Republic, Old Navy, and Gap Outlet.

- The trade name is the name on the storefront sign and on the store's advertising. The corporate name is the name of the retail enterprise that owns and operates the stores.

Core Concepts

✓ Lease exhibits
✓ Description of premises should not be lease plan
✓ Adjacencies
✓ Avoid co-tenancy

DESCRIPTION OF THE LEASED PREMISES

The lease will typically state the width and depth of the space, the area in square feet and the space number or street number and address.

Because it is not easy to describe the property in surveyor's terms, it may be *more* useful to attach a page to the lease marking the exact space in which the tenant's premises are located. Attaching separate pages at the end of the lease document to fully explain special details is an accepted practice. These attachments are commonly called exhibits or addenda.

The proper exhibit should depict the layout of the shopping center with the tenant's demised premises highlighted in blockout form without the names of adjacent tenants so as not to imply co-tenancy.

As a word of caution, showing inaccurate information about the sizes and names of other stores on the attached exhibit page may be costly. For example, tenants who want to be released from a lease obligation could claim that the landlord promised that the anchor stores named on the exhibit page would operate in the center. Lease plans should never be used as exhibits on the lease for this reason.

Core Concepts

✓ Lease commencement date not same as rent commencement date

✓ Non-monetary obligations

COMMENCEMENT DATE

Generally, tenants do not want to pay rent until they open and start doing business, regardless of how long it takes to build out or construct their space. On the other hand, landlords rely on cash flow from the center. To resolve these separate interests, the rent commencement date can be set on the earlier to occur of the date the tenant opens for business, a set number of days after delivery to and possession of the space by the tenant, or a set number of days after the lease is fully executed.

Sometimes a tenant is given an incentive to open sooner. For example, if the shopping center is newly constructed and planning a grand opening, tenants that open before the 60-day period might be rewarded with a period of abated minimum rent or percentage rent.

Additional Tenant Obligations

When possession of the premises is taken, regardless of the rent commencement date, tenants may be obligated to non-monetary requirements:

- Provide the certificates of insurance required by the lease, dated from the day the premises are accepted.
- Sign an acceptance of the premises letter confirming the date of occupancy and the condition of the space.
- Honor all provisions of the lease agreement.

The above non-monetary obligations usually occur on the *lease commencement date*, whereas monetary obligations occur upon *rent commencement date*. The lease commencement date is often a date on which the landlord delivers possession of the leased premises with the landlord's work substantially completed.

Core Concepts

✓ Lease expiration can be different from lease termination date through legal action

✓ Lease should state exact date of termination

TERMINATION DATE

t is important to name a specific date of lease termination. For example, rather than stating only that the lease shall terminate 60 months from the lease commencement date, it may be beneficial to calculate and record the specific month and date of termination. Many retailers prefer that their leases terminate at the same time as the other stores they operate. January 31 is a common lease date because it gives retailers a full Christmas season of November and December and an extra month to clear away merchandise or renovate if the lease is renewed. Sometimes the lease can be terminated through legal action before the stated lease expiration date.

Core Concepts

✓ Consider amortization of improvements
✓ Factors influence lease term
✓ Options

LEASE TERM

Generally, the cost of tenant build-out (the total cost of the construction of the space the tenant occupies) must be amortized over a lease term (length of lease) and consistent with generally accepted accounting principles (GAAP). If construction expenses are considerable for either the tenant or the landlord, the lease term may tend to be longer. Consider all factors of importance to the landlord and tenant when setting the lease term. Small shop space is usually between five and fifteen years with no options. Anchor space uses a longer lease term and sometimes has one or more options for renewal.

Core Concepts

✓ "Extend term" is preferable than "lease renewed"

✓ Effect of options on economics of the center

✓ Exclude option rights if lease is assigned

LEASE RENEWAL OPTIONS

A renewal option is a provision that permits tenants to extend the terms of their original leases. If tenants choose to exercise options, they may make a dramatic impact on the future income stream of the shopping center, as the landlord is being asked to speculate as to potential future rents. An option prearranges the terms under which a lease renewal may occur. Without an option, the tenant must negotiate new economic terms and often an entirely new lease with the landlord. Use of the language "the term may be extended" rather than "the lease may be renewed" may help avoid the question of applicability of original lease covenants in the extended term.

Assignees

The option is typically personal to a specific tenant. No assignee—a new tenant who assumes the rights and responsibilities of the original tenant—should be able to exercise an option. It is not usually in the landlord's best interest to permit an assignee to renew a lease. This is an opportunity for the landlord to negotiate a new lease with the assignee or to lease to a new tenant.

> # Core Concepts
>
> ✓ Independent covenant
> ✓ Additional rents
> ✓ Difference between overage and percentage rent
> ✓ Natural and artificial breakpoints

RENT

Typically, two basic types of rent are charged in connection with the lease—minimum rent and percentage rent. Rent should be an independent covenant in the lease. This means that if the landlord defaults for any reason, the tenant must still pay the rent. Lenders often require this provision to protect the cash flow of the center. A third type of rent is known as additional rents or extra charges.

Minimum Rent

Minimum rent is generally stated in an annual amount and divided into monthly installments due and payable on the first of the month. If you agree to a "grace period," it may be a good idea to try to limit the frequency of late payment of rent. For example, the landlord might agree to no more than two late payments in a 12-month period.

Percentage Rent

Some leases require no minimum or base rent to be paid, only percentage rent. That is a certain percentage of the tenant's sales. Other leases are structured so the tenant is obligated to pay a minimum rent and a percentage of sales if a sales threshold is achieved. The portion of percentage rent over the minimum rent paid is known as overage rent.

The shopping center landlord takes a percentage of the tenant's gross sales over a breakpoint. A natural breakpoint is a sales threshold that determines the point at which overage rent is paid, and it is often established by dividing the fixed minimum rent to be paid by the tenant by the percentage. For example, $50,000/6% = $833,333. Breakpoints may be set arbitrarily by lease agreement. These are called artificial or unnatural breakpoints.

Overage rent may be paid in a variety of ways. One is when sales for each month exceed one-twelfth of the breakpoint. For example, if the breakpoint is $1.2 million annually, in January, as soon as the tenant reaches more than $100,000 ($1/12$), the tenant will begin paying the agreed-upon percentage rent.

Core Concepts

- ✓ Landlord pays costs associated with relocation
- ✓ New location should be acceptable to tenant

RELOCATION CLAUSE

This provision gives the landlord the right to move a tenant within the shopping center. It could be important in a new shopping center when the center's leasing plan may be subject to change prior to building the center. If a center is undergoing a redevelopment, a relocation clause is also desirable for similar reasons. Typically, the new site is a location mutually acceptable to both the landlord and the tenant. Often, if the landlord requires the tenant to move, the landlord pays for all or a portion of the moving expenses.

Core Concepts

✓ Kick-out can be at tenant's option, landlord's option or mutual

✓ Right to terminate

KICK-OUT CLAUSE

This provision gives the landlord the option to terminate the tenant's lease if the tenant does not reach percentage rent during some specified period in the term of the lease. A common time period for a *kick-out* clause would be three years. The sophisticated tenant may argue that this should be mutual. Rather than making the provision mutual, landlords sometimes omit it altogether, because tenants could in theory control their sales, and accordingly, this provision could give tenants a way to terminate their leases. A kick-out provision in the lease is more formally referred to as *right to terminate*.

Core Concepts

✓ Specific language recommended for use of premises

✓ Limit the use

✓ Landlord was restricted, tenant wants flexibility

✓ Exclusives

PERMITTED USE

A *permitted use* clause defines what type of business may operate on the premises and which types of products the business may sell or services offered. It is very important to delineate in the lease exactly how the space will be used. It is also critical that a future tenant who sublets the space be bound to the identical original use clause. For example, a "drug store" can be a small pharmacy or a huge cosmetic retailer without a pharmacy. You must describe exactly what goods may be sold on the premises, and you must use the word "only." For example, a correct bakery use clause may permit the sale of baked goods *only*. Be specific. Do not state "may carry women's apparel and related items." Typically, the landlord will want the permitted use provision to be as restrictive as possible, whereas the tenant will want as much flexibility as possible due to possible changes in the future to the nature of its operation.

Exclusive Rights and Antitrust

To prohibit competition, tenants will sometimes request an exclusive right to sell certain goods in the shopping center. Landlords should be careful before granting these clauses. One problem, among many, in granting an exclusive is that it may violate antitrust laws.

To help avoid antitrust problems, a use clause should be narrow in scope, reasonably limiting the type of goods sold within a premises. Central issues in antitrust law violation include:

- The concept of reasonableness: Is it a reasonable restraint of trade?
- The term of an exclusive: Is it an indefinite period or is it a five-year term?
- The character of the business excluded: Is a men's store excluded or only suits?

By granting *exclusives* the landlord takes on an implied responsibility to "police" the merchandise sold by the rest of the tenants. The landlord also risks not being flexible with national tenants that often use product extension throughout their chain of stores to respond to trends and as a way to grow their business.

Core Concepts

✓ Violation of radius restrictions results in monetary penalty
✓ Violation of radius restrictions dilutes tenant sales, affecting overage rent

RADIUS RESTRICTION

This provision prevents a tenant from opening a store nearby, or within a specified radius of the center, without permission from the landlord. Such a restriction prevents tenants from dividing their businesses and thus lowering the percentage rent paid to the landlord and encouraging shoppers to go to the store with lower percentage rent. This clause may also present antitrust issues.

Following are examples of satisfactory compromises by the landlord in negotiating this lease provision.

■ Does not restrain competition but agrees to have the tenant report the sales of any store the tenant opens within the radius restriction and have those sales combined with the tenant's reported sales subject to overage rent.

- Permits another trade name for a store within the restricted retail area
- Limits the restraint to a specified time period.
- Places a monetary penalty for violating radius restrictions.

Core Concepts

✓ Exhibits are incorporated as part of the lease document
✓ Lengthy documents
✓ Legal description

LEASE EXHIBITS

L ease exhibits—attachments to an original lease—are an important part of the lease and require careful review. Exhibits, which are normally lengthy and detailed, may include:

- A legal description of the center.
- A site plan (a generalized document only, a pictorial representation of the location of the leased premises).
- A construction exhibit that includes descriptions of the construction work performed by the landlord and tenant.

Core Concepts

✓ Gross receipts
✓ Inclusions and exclusions from gross receipts
✓ Sales reporting

GROSS SALES

The landlord will want a very broad definition of gross sales; that is, the sales which are included in determining the percentage rent and overage rent a tenant will pay. This is also stated in leases as gross receipts. The concept is that the landlord expects every dollar the demised premises generates to be used in calculating percentage rent owed. This may include such items as purchases made on vending machines, a customer phoning in an order and a customer who comes into the store and orders merchandise that is later delivered from the warehouse. Generally, the tenant may not want the computation of gross receipts to include the following:

■ Sales tax: It is not retained by the tenant.

- Bad debt expense: If the tenant does not collect the sale, it should not be included.
- Credit card company charges: It is not ever collected by the tenant.
- Services: A clothing retailer, for example, may provide wardrobe consultation services and gift wrapping as a convenience for its customers. The store plans only to break even on these services, not to profit from them. Therefore, the retailer may claim that sales collected from these endeavors should be exempt from gross receipts calculation.

Core Concepts

✓ Who pays for tenant audit
✓ Where audit is conducted

RIGHT TO AUDIT

An audit right is tied directly to the definition of gross sales and to the percentage rent concept. The landlord must verify that the tenant pays the accurate amount of rent as percentage rent and/or overage rent based on the gross receipts the store generated. If a landlord has reason to believe that the tenant is not paying what is owed, the landlord must have an avenue to determine if the rent paid is accurate. Among the options:

- A landlord must have the right to have the tenant's accounting records audited, even in the middle of the lease year.
- If the landlord cannot audit on the premises, the tenant may be required to send the records to the landlord.

■ The tenant must send financial statements. Usually, certified statements by an outside certified public accountant or the firm's chief financial officer are acceptable. The financial statements should include a year-end statement and typically a monthly gross sales statement.

Audit Results

Usually, if an audit discloses that the tenant had underreported gross receipts through an error that resulted in underpayment of percentage rent of more than a certain percentage, for example 3%, the tenant must pay all audit costs. A specified exception for clerical error is included in many lease clauses.

Sometimes the deliberate nonpayment of percentage rent constitutes a default in the lease.

Core Concepts

✓ Parking ratio
✓ Employee parking
✓ Definition of common areas

COMMON AREAS

Generally, "areas and facilities of common benefit to the tenants and occupants of the landlord's site" are defined as common areas. Common areas include sidewalks, interior mall corridors, fire corridors, service areas, parking areas, landscaped areas, and retention pond as well as areas that are a part of the building, such as the roof, ceilings, etc. Three common areas that tenants sometimes question concern kiosks, parking and repairs.

Kiosks

Kiosks are temporary or permanent additions to the common areas of a shopping center complex used for leasing purposes.

The addition of kiosks to a shopping center may create an access or visibility problem for existing tenants. If adding a kiosk hinders a potential customer's access to or view of a tenant's storefront, the tenant usually makes a complaint. Common remedies for a tenant in this situation include:

- The tenant's right to terminate the lease if sales drop by a certain percentage (if tenant has a "kick-out" clause in its lease)
- Rent abatement.

Center Parking

In order to comply with zoning requirements, a shopping center must usually maintain a certain number of parking spaces relative to its size. The common ratio is five parking spaces per 1,000 square feet of gross leasable area. Different uses other than retail, such as movie theatres, may require different ratios. Some mass merchants require as much as eight parking spaces per 1,000 square feet of gross leasable area and immediately in front of its store. For tenants this means:

- Requiring that landlords comply with the applicable zoning requirements
- Having employees, generally, park in the remote areas of the parking lot to assure convenient parking for shoppers. (This may be difficult to police.)

Repairs

It is important, especially in a new center or a center planned for redevelopment, to make certain that the landlord has the right to make repairs to the common areas, including the right to close an entrance to the center for repairs. Sometimes a tenant will receive a rent reduction or be permitted to pay only percentage rent for this inconvenience. In addition to closing an entrance, the landlord must maintain flexibility in order to:

- Change or add buildings, parking and common areas.
- Maintain the landlord's pipes and ducts through the tenant's space.
- Care for the roof and exterior walls of the premises.

Core Concepts

✓ CAM caps
✓ Leasable area vs. leased area
✓ Operating costs
✓ Definition of pro rata
✓ Tenant audit rights
✓ Flat CAM

COMMON AREA MAINTENANCE (CAM) AND OPERATING COSTS

Generally, operating costs include the tenant's share of *common area maintenance* (CAM) and insurance applicable to the common areas. The landlord wants a very broad definition of common area maintenance. One item often excluded from the CAM charges is capital expenses, that is, terms that can be depreciated over a useful life and that improve the value of the property. However, even capital expenditure recoveries depend upon lease language. Additional operating costs include, without limitation, the total cost of operating, repairing, replacing, lighting, cleaning, landscaping, maintaining, painting, securing (if landlord shall so elect to do so), managing administration of and insuring the shopping center. Additionally, costs incurred in complying with governmental laws, ordinances, codes, rules and regulations are also recoverable under the CAM operating costs umbrella.

Pro Rata Share

It is in the tenant's best interest to base the calculation of tenants' pro rata or proportionate share on the center's total *leasable area* by square footage. It is in the landlord's best interest to use the total leased area as opposed to the leasable area as the denominator when computing the tenants' pro rata share of CAM. Under the leasable area scenario, the landlord is responsible to pay the pro rata share of CAM for vacant space, whereas on the leased scenario, tenants pick up the entire operating costs except where CAM caps exist. For example, in a center newly leased:

- The tenant will advocate the computation 5,000 sq. ft. divided by 100,000 sq. ft. (total leasable area) = 5%.
- The landlord will advocate the computation 5,000 sq. ft. divided by 50,000 sq. ft. (total leased area) = 10%.

Common compromises include:

- The tenant never having to bear more than 80% of the total area
- Caps on the common area charges.

How CAM Charges Are Paid

Usually CAM charges are paid monthly, in advance, at the time of minimum rental payment. If the actual CAM charges exceed the estimated charges that the tenant paid throughout the year, the landlord will assess the tenant for the additional amount to be paid as rent. This is known as CAM adjustment billings. If the actual CAM charges are less than the estimated charges, the landlord will credit or refund the necessary amount to the tenant.

In older centers, the common area charges are easily predicted through the landlord budgeting process except variable items such as snow removal, which varies by winter precipitation. In new centers, common area expense predictions can cause misunderstandings if the rates are much higher than rates represented in lease negotiations prior to the center experiencing a full year of operation. Therefore, it is important to use care in estimating these charges.

A ceiling on charges may be a bad idea because of the unpredictability of future changes in expenses. In addition to snow removal, fluctuations can occur in energy and insurance. As the center matures and warranty on major areas and equipment expires, costs will escalate. These include roofs, parking lots and HVAC equipment.

In accounting procedures, use care in determining what costs are attributed to the tenant. Do not double-count items. Sometimes a tenant will demand the right to audit the landlord's books to justify their extra charges such as real estate taxes and pass-through expenses. Use care when granting this right in a lease. Some landlords will use an independent auditing firm to audit their charges so as to provide the tenants with a third-party certification of these charges.

Some leases require the tenant to pay a flat amount as the total contribution to CAM in addition to or as part of minimum rent.

Core Concepts

- ✓ Merchants' association
- ✓ Marketing fund
- ✓ Participation requirement
- ✓ Tenant cost

MARKETING, ADVERTISING AND PROMOTIONS

Typically, this provision requires a tenant to spend a certain amount of money on advertising the store during the year. This provision may further require that tenants participate in shopping center promotions and sponsored advertising a certain number of times each year. Lastly, there may be a marketing fund fee associated with a merchants' association or a marketing fund. The marketing, advertising and promotions provision of the lease is based on the premise that it is in the best interest of both tenant and landlord to market, advertise and promote the shopping center and as such, this provision requires this tenant cost to be considered as additional rent. The amount the tenant is charged is usually a per-square-

foot fee that may be adjusted annually. The funds are adminis-
tered in one of two ways:

- A merchants' association is a group formed of merchants
  who elect a president and generally organize promotions and
  cooperative advertising for the benefit of the entire center.
- A marketing fund is generally operated by the landlord
  on behalf of the tenants in an attempt to maximize the
  sales of the shopping center.

Core Concepts

✓ Costs for monitoring and contesting assessments

✓ Real estate tax language is broad to include public charges and assessments

✓ Triple net lease

PAYMENT OF TAXES AND INSURANCE

Generally, tenants will pay the pro rata share of real estate taxes and insurance (see Pro Rata Share, above).

Tenants will pay their pro rata share of real estate taxes. However, tenants do not pay the landlord's income tax. Keep in mind:

- Other than an attempt to be competitive in the market-place, generally there is little incentive to contest real estate taxes unless the tenant is willing to pay for costs associated with the contest, because the tenant realizes the sole benefit from this action. Some leases allow the landlord to be reimbursed by the tenants for legal and other costs associated with monitoring and contesting property and land assessments for the purpose of levying property taxes.

Real estate tax is computed as follows:

■ Assessment may be made from the date of commencement of the lease or assessment may be made from a base period. For example, the shopping center may agree to pay all taxes until the base year 2005. All increases after 2005 will be paid by the tenant. The tenant will generally insist that it pay only installments that are payable during the term of the lease.

Language in a Lease Clause

Particular language may be included in a lease, such as:

■ A provision for a new or different tax: For example, an environmental tax based on parking spaces, or calling the real estate tax by another name.

■ A provision for assessing the tenant for a tax contest initiated by the landlord: The rationale for this is that the tenant benefits from a reduction of taxes.

■ If the tenant pays all the insurance, taxes and common area maintenance, the lease would be considered a triple net lease. Insurance is often included in CAM for pro rata reimbursement by tenants.

Core Concepts

✓ Right of entry
✓ For Lease signs
✓ Emergency repairs
✓ Rent shall not abate while premises are being repaired

LANDLORD'S ACCESS TO PREMISES

The landlord must have the right to enter the tenant's space at any time to make repairs or alterations, both to the center and for other tenants (for example, runs for utility lines) and always in an emergency, without incurring any costs. For example, if the landlord must break the front lock in order to enter a store to prevent water damage to premises and contents from sprinklers that have accidentally gone off, the tenant should be responsible for the repair cost of the broken lock. Furthermore, the landlord may want the right to show the tenant's space during the last year of the lease or during the six months prior to the expiration of the lease term. Some leases may allow the landlord to place a "For Lease" sign on the tenant's premises during the six months prior to lease expiration date.

Core Concepts

✓ Tenant installation

✓ "Trade fixtures" are not "tenant improvements"

TRADE FIXTURES REMOVAL

The tenant should, at the tenant's sole cost and expense, repair or refit the premises at termination of the lease. For example, the cost of removing unusual or large fixtures, such as safes in jewelry stores or in savings and loans offices, should be borne by the tenant. If the tenant fails, the landlord may pursue the tenant for reimbursement of the cost.

Conversely, the tenant is required to install all trade fixtures and equipment required to operate the business. The term *trade fixtures* typically does not include carpeting, floor covering, attached shelving, lighting fixtures (other than free-standing lamps), wall coverings, ceilings, and other similar *tenant improvements*, which become the property of the landlord upon surrender of the premises by the tenant upon lease termination.

Core Concepts

✓ Assignment and subletting
require landlord consent

✓ Assignment transfers rights
and obligations

✓ Change of control may
allow assignments involving
mergers and acquisitions

ASSIGNMENT AND SUBLETTING

The legal distinctions between an assignment and a sub-lease of the premises follow:

- An assignment is a transfer of the lease rights and obligations from the original tenant to a new tenant. An assignment of lease practically holds the new tenant entirely responsible for upholding the lease terms; however, the original tenant may also remain liable unless the parties agree to the contrary.

- A sublease between the tenant and a subtenant does not convey privity of contract or privity of estate with the landlord. In other words, the subtenant in this case has no contractual rights or obligations with respect to the original landlord. The subtenant's obligation rests with the original tenant named in the lease, who remains the tenant of the landlord. In the event a tenant sublets and the landlord approves, the subtenant is nevertheless required by the landlord to abide by the obligations of the original lease, such as permitted use, and the tenant is responsible for enforcing such obligations upon the subtenant.

The landlord almost never gives a tenant an unfettered right to assign the lease or sublet the premises. Usually there is no assignment or subletting without the landlord's consent, which the landlord covenants not to withhold unreasonably.

Change of Control

This section softens prohibition against assignment and subletting by permitting the tenant to assign to a subsidiary or a corporation into which the tenant is merged or acquired so long as the transferee agrees to continue to operate the business under the approved trade name.

Core Concepts

✓ New forms of utilities: cable, satellite, Wi-Fi, wireless Internet, cellular

✓ Reselling utilities to tenants

UTILITIES

I t is customary for the tenant to be responsible for applying for, obtaining, and paying for all utilities that it consumes. These utilities include, but are not limited to, electricity, gas, water (for domestic use, fire protection, and if space includes exterior landscaping, for irrigation), telephone, cable, high-speed Internet or Wi-Fi wireless Internet, satellite, garbage collection, and HVAC services.

Generally, landlords work with utilities in the following ways:

- Direct tenant hookup with utility companies: In this case, landlords will not assume any responsibility for the utilities and, therefore, even if the utility stops service, tenants are liable for their rent. Utility covenants are independent covenants. For example, if tenant experiences a power failure, the lease still maintains that the tenant must operate and pay rent, regardless of habitability of the premises. Practically speaking, landlords usually work with the tenant in unusual circumstances that affect the tenant's ability to operate in the leased premises.

- As a profit center or a break-even operation, so long as laws and ordinances permit it. As a condition, landlords must be certain they can provide utilities before making a lease covenant that obligates them to do so. A landlord wants to be able to discontinue providing utility services on short notice without liability providing there is major retrofit of utility of lines that would make the change prohibitive.

Central Plant Operation

The tenant should agree to pay a heating and cooling charge in accordance with a schedule normally prepared by heating and cooling engineers. In this covenant the following should be considered:

- A detailed method for developing an annual base rate or fee.
- A detailed basis for an adjustment. Specifically, the basis for adjustments includes normal cost increases for utility fees, materials and labor, including fringe benefits in the calculation of wages.
- Whether tenant will pay and receive cooled or heated air; or chilled water or steam, to use as part of its own system.

Core Concepts

✓ Prevents undue interference by landlord

✓ Obligates tenant to comply with lease obligations to receive benefit of quiet enjoyment

QUIET ENJOYMENT

A quiet enjoyment provision is a kind of landlord nondisturbance agreement. It is a covenant that the tenant will not be evicted because the landlord does not have good title or full rights to lease the property for the term.

As a matter of law, a landlord is estopped from interfering with a tenant's occupation, operation, and possession of the demised premises. This tenant right is implied—whether or not stated by this clause—as landlord covenants that the tenant, upon paying all sums due and performing all tenant's obligations under the lease, shall peacefully and quietly have, hold and enjoy the leased premises without undue interference by the landlord.

Core Concepts

✓ Foreclosure would require tenant to attorn

✓ Tenants whose leases subordinate to a mortgagee want nondisturbance agreement

✓ Nondisturbance allow tenant quiet enjoyment if no defaults occur in event of foreclosures

ATTORNMENT, SUBORDINATION AND NONDISTURBANCE

The landlord's lender usually requires the tenant to agree to by lease to attorn to the mortgagee if the mortgagee were to foreclose, the result of which would be for the tenant to recognize the mortgagee or its assigns as the new landlord in that event.

A subordination/nondisturbance agreement is important to the landlord as well, because if the tenant's lease is superior to the landlord's mortgage, a purchaser will make an offer expecting to receive the current rents from all existing tenants. For example, if the lease is made at a rent that is lower than the current market's, the lender cannot arbitrarily terminate the lease in order to re-lease the premises for a higher rate. However, if the tenant's lease is subordinate to the landlord's and no subordination-nondisturbance agreement is executed and recorded with the County Recorder's Office, the tenant's lease may be renegotiated or terminated when the property is sold.

- Subordination: There is a hierarchy of rents to the property that is based on factors such as possession of the property and recording of documents. The lender may want to have the highest priority. If a tenant agrees to subordinate, the tenant is agreeing to give up its higher priority for a lesser priority.
- Nondisturbance agreement: In return for agreeing to subordinate, the tenant may require the lender to enter into a nondisturbance agreement providing that so long as the tenant is not in default under the lease, the lender will not disturb the tenant's possession of the premises whether or not following a foreclosure.

Core Concepts

✓ Estoppel certificates certify if defaults exist and if lease is in force and effect

✓ Failure to note default in certificates estops tenant from making such claims against mortgagee or new landlord

ESTOPPEL

An estoppel is a written document that is an agreement between the landlord and the tenant (sometimes the lender) of the center specifying details of the lease and premises at a given point in time. It is important to understand the following points:

- The purpose of an estoppel is to outline in advance exactly what the terms of the lease situation are and to outline any and all claims that the parties may have against one another.
- Usually an estoppel is obtained before the purchase, sale or refinancing of a property.
- A defect or claim should be specified in an estoppel certificate; otherwise the tenant may not have a claim against

a new landlord. Similarly, the new landlord may some-times find it difficult to pursue a problem that the past landlord initiated.

■ An estoppel lease clause is absolutely indispensable to any landlord because a prospective lender or purchaser of the shopping center will always require estoppel certificates from tenants stating whether the lease is in full force and effect or if there are defaults on the part of the landlord. The failure of the tenant to specify landlord defaults in an estoppel certificate will estop the tenant from asserting such past defaults against the new mortgagee or the land-lord in the future.

Core Concepts

✓ Tenants want their responsibilities specified and the landlord responsible for everything else

✓ Landlords want their responsibilities specified and the tenant responsible for everything else

REPAIRS

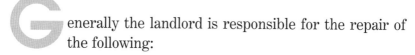 enerally the landlord is responsible for the repair of the following:

- The structural elements of the building, including exterior supporting walls and foundation
- The roof, downspouts and gutters
- The common area of the building

Typically the tenant wants this covenant expanded if possible. For example, the tenant may claim that the landlord should be responsible for "faults" if the landlord does the build-out or other flaws that are present in the premises. Landlords will seek to limit or restrain their liability.

Core Concepts

✓ Operating covenant
✓ Prevents store from closing and just paying rent
✓ Liquidated damages

CONTINUOUS OCCUPANCY CLAUSE

A continuous occupancy clause, or operating covenant, is of crucial importance in a lease document. The landlord wants to be assured that the tenant will be open and operating and that the store will have merchandise available for purchase during the shopping center's normal hours.

Also, the landlord may require that tenants' windows be lighted when the center is open to shoppers and to visitors for a specified time after normal shopping and working hours. When a center is full of customers, a dark store conveys a bad image for the entire shopping center.

If a tenant closes early, the landlord may insist on *liquidated damages* (payments of an agreed-upon amount for breaching their contract), not as a penalty but as an actual estimate of damages. For example, if you are dealing with a major store or an anchor tenant, calculating the percentage rent lost to the landlord as a result of the store's closing is extremely difficult. A liquidated damages clause is an attempt to approximate this liability in advance.

Core Concepts

✓ Landlord enforcement
✓ Specific action

SPECIFIC PERFORMANCE

f a covenant of the lease is breached, a specific performance clause provides that the landlord may seek a court order for the tenant to comply with a specific action.

Core Concepts

✓ Remedy and costs of noncompliance

✓ Monetary damages deter tenant from lease violations that become unenforceable

DAMAGES

As an alternative or in addition to specific performance a party may seek damages. A damages clause outlines a future, specific remedy and the costs of noncompliance with a provision. If, for example, the tenant's lease has expired, the tenant and the landlord fail to reach an agreement on a new lease and the tenant refuses to close the store and vacate the premises, the landlord could claim that the tenant owes holdover rent—perhaps plus a penalty equal to 150% or 200% above the original rent—if it was specified in advance. Keep the following points in mind:

- Damages that approximate the landlord's loss are generally acceptable.

■ Damages that are excessive probably will not hold up in court.

For example, late charges are generally acceptable and collectable if fees are reasonable and charges not exorbitant.

Core Concepts

✓ Grace period to cure default
✓ Remedy

RIGHT TO CURE DEFAULTS

The landlord must have the ability to step in for a tenant and resolve a default that the tenant has created. This is especially important for the landlord in cases where a tenant may have created a potential hazard for the shopping center—for example, a restaurant tenant that does not maintain its exhaust fan free of grease (a potential fire hazard). Also, if the tenant does not pay insurance, the landlord has the right to buy insurance and to charge the tenant for it as part of the tenant's additional rent. Some leases will give the tenant five (5) days' grace period to cure a default in the payment of rent and thirty (30) days' grace period to cure nonmonetary defaults.

Core Concepts

✓ Significant landlord rules for tenants should be in the lease

✓ Control deliveries to tenants

✓ Employee parking

✓ Prevent noise in common area

OPERATING RULES

Delivery or shipment of merchandise, supplies and fixtures to and from the premises; loading and unloading of goods; garbage and refuse disposal and handling; the prohibition of using loudspeakers or sound equipment that can be heard from the common area; the use of pest extermination contracts by the tenant and provisions for tenant employee parking are among landlord operating rules commonly found in a lease article under a section titled Operating Rules and Regulations. The tenant generally is required to keep the premises neat at all times, and deliveries must be made at the back of the premises if possible. It is important to control deliveries in order to maintain the physical appearance of the property and safety of customers.

Core Concepts

✓ Tenant responsibility for complying with new code requirements

COMPLIANCE WITH LAW

Tenants must comply with the law, local ordinance, code, etc. while operating their stores in the shopping center. For example, sprinklers are required in most buildings used for commercial activity. However, this may be a new ordinance or code. In order to comply with a new law, the tenant must pay to install the required fixtures in its leased premises that may not have sprinklers. Although these costs can never be predicted, it is the tenant's risk and a cost of doing business.

Core Concepts

✓ Mechanic's liens
✓ Waiver of the right to file liens
✓ Nonresponsibility notices

TENANT SHALL DISCHARGE LIENS

enants must pay their bills promptly. This is of special concern to the landlord, especially in the case of work done by the tenant to improve the lease premises that could result in a lien. For example, if subcontractors are not paid, a mechanic's lien can be placed on the property, giving rights to foreclose on the property to collect the amount of the debt. If liens are placed on the property, landlords would probably violate the terms of their mortgages with their lenders, which could place them in jeopardy of foreclosure by the lender as well.

Lease language should provide for tenant to discharge any lien (including those of mechanics, laborers, and materialmen) for work done in the leased premises. In most U.S. jurisdictions, a statutory lien is created in favor of mechanics or workers that perform work on real estate and material contractors who supply material for such work, e.g. carpet installation. The liens arise irrespective of whether work is done on leased premises or common area. Landlords sometimes post notices of nonresponsibility for liens in leased premises under construction to encourage contractors to settle matters of payment for work and material directly with the tenant.

Core Concepts

✓ Hold harmless agreements
✓ Indemnify
✓ Defend

INDEMNIFICATION

Generally, the landlord and tenant agree in advance to mutually indemnify each other. In other words, they agree that if one party is brought into or made part of an action as a result of its relationship with the other party, the party who is responsible will bear the costs of defense and any associated liability. For example, the landlord seeks to have a tenant look to its own insurance carrier for damages if the roof leaks. The landlord does not want to pay for the tenant's merchandise. Any claim would raise the cost of the landlord's insurance, which might put the landlord at a competitive disadvantage. Some lease clauses will provide that the tenant will defend, indemnify and hold landlord harmless for claims made of the landlord resulting from incidents involving the leased premises.

Core Concepts

✓ Mutual release
✓ Subrogation

MUTUAL WAIVER OF SUBROGATION

A mutual waiver of subrogation is an issue related to indemnification. A waiver of subrogation means that the insurance company of a party who suffers a loss such as by a fire in the center will not sue the party at fault. The insurance company of the party not at fault waives its right to step into the shoes of the insured to bring suit against someone. Instead, each insurance company compensates its insured.

The purpose of this section in the lease is to place the burden on each party's property insurer.

Core Concepts

✓ Conveyance of real property
✓ Contract law
✓ Responsibilities, obligations and rights

PURPOSE OF THE LEASE

Legally, a lease is a conveyance of real property that is governed by general property law, and it serves as a contract, with provisions governed by general contract law. The purpose of a lease is to allocate risk among the parties involved: It outlines the responsibilities and obligations of the parties and provides solutions to issues. The language involved here includes such matters as letters of intent, lease forms, terms, renewal options, assignment and subletting, use rights and restrictions, audits, tax payments, utilities and estoppel. The parties involved in shopping center leases generally are the landlord, the tenant and the lender. And because the center manager typically resolves ambiguities that may arise in a lease, it is critical that the manager be familiar with the language of the lease.

Glossary

The glossary that follows is a listing of key definitions compiled from this outline, with several terms not defined in the outline added for your information. The terms are defined within the context of this shopping center management topic.

Addendum   Lease change or addition usually inserted at the end of the original lease form.

Antitrust violation   Participation in the restriction of trade or commerce.

Assignee   New tenant that assumes the rights and responsibilities of the original tenant.

Assignment   Transfer by the tenant of all tenant's obligations and rights to a new entity.

Audit   Ability of one party to examine the books and accounting records of the other, usually for the purpose of verifying percentage rent or common area charges.

Certificates of insurance   Documents that show proof of insurance.

Commencement date   Day on which tenant's lease term begins, not to be confused with occupancy date or rent commencement date.

Common area maintenance (CAM) charges Charges shared among tenants for landlord's maintenance and operation of common areas.

Consideration Something tangible, usually money, that has been promised or done that binds a legal obligation and makes it enforceable.

Construction allowance Money given to tenant for completion of tenant build-out. Also known as tenant improvement (TI) allowance.

Continuous occupancy clause A requirement to fully operate a store during mall hours without interruption or closing. Prevents tenant from closing store and paying rent.

Default Failure to comply with terms of the lease.

Estoppel certificate Tenant or landlord represents as to the current relationship of the tenant and landlord, that is, an estoppel certificate will set forth whether there are any defaults or whether rent has been paid in advance. This document would have each party agree that the lease is in full force and effect and that no covenant is breached.

Exclusive rights Guarantee that a specific category of merchandise will be sold only by a certain store.

Exhibits Attachments, usually toward the end of an original lease, specifying site location, legal description and tenant's construction specifications.

Expiration date Date on which tenant's lease term ends. Also known as lease termination date.

Flat CAM A fixed tenant-occupancy charge in addition to base minimum rent, which may include nearly all additional costs, such as marketing and CAM. Excluded may be insurance, utilities, and real estate taxes, which are not usually under the landlord's control. Flat CAM may be escalated on an annual agreed upon rate such as the Consumer Price Index (CPI).

Gross sales Total sales from all transactions minus exclusions agreed in the lease subject to percentage rent provisions. Also known as gross receipts.

Guaranty Assurance of performance by one party of another party's obligation.

Hold harmless A promise by one party not to hold the other party responsible if the other party carries out the contract in a way that causes damage to the first party. In leases, tenants generally agree not to sue the landlord if tenant's property is damaged due to landlord's failure to maintain the premises.

Indemnification Protection against suit or expenses. See hold harmless.

Kick-out clause Option that allows a landlord or tenant to terminate the lease before the end of the term.

Lease   A transfer of use or occupancy rights for a given period or term.

Letter of intent   Generally a nonbinding document in most U.S. jurisdictions submitted prior to a formal lease. It serves to delineate the intentions between the landlord and the tenant. Basic issues, including minimum rent, percentage rent, pass-through expenses and other major points of negotiation, are outlined.

Liability   Legal obligation or responsibility.

Liquidated damages   Payments of an agreed-upon amount for the breaching of a contract.

Minimum rent   Rent that is not based on tenant's sales. Also known as fixed minimum rent and base rent.

Nondisturbance covenant   Usually gives tenant assurance of continuous operation of its store in the event of landlord's foreclosure.

Overage rent   Percentage rent paid as a percentage of sales exceeding a breakpoint.

Pass-through expenses   Tenant's portion of expense composed of common area maintenance, taxes and insurance and any other expenses determined by landlord to be paid by tenant.

Percentage rent   Rent based upon a percentage of tenant's sales. When paid in addition to a minimum or base rent, is referred to as overage rent.

Pro rata share   Assessment of expenses on a proportional basis of space so designated in the shopping center.

Quiet enjoyment clause   Gives tenant assurance that landlord will not interfere with tenants right to operate its business in the leased premises, provided no defaults exist.

Radius restriction   Specific trade radius in which tenant may not operate another business, usually of the same type or name.

Relocation clause   Gives landlord the ability to move the tenant to another location within the shopping center premises.

Renewal option   Agreement at the time of the original lease as to terms of tenant's extension of lease term.

Specific performance clause   Gives one party the right to cause another party to comply with the lease.

Sublet   Original tenant remains liable for the lease while a new subtenant assumes occupancy.

Subordination clause   Defines whether tenant or landlord obligations are recognized first in the case of foreclosure or sale of the property.

Termination   The lease termination date is a date on the lease when the term expires. Interruption of the lease before the term expires is sometimes referred to as termination.

Trade name   Name under which tenant operates a business.

Trade fixture   Item specific to a tenant's business, usually not attached to the walls or floor; usually removed at lease expiration.

Use clause   Outline of the exact type of merchandise to be sold or business to be conducted in the premises. Also known as permitted use.

Waiver of subrogation   Each party to the lease gives up the right for its insurer to bring suit against the other party's insurer.